One Rehearsal Christmas Plays

Preschool through Middle School

NEXGEN®

Building the New Generation of Believers

An Imprint of Cook Communications Ministries
COLORADO SPRINGS, COLORADO • PARIS, ONTARIO
KINGSWAY COMMUNICATIONS, LTD., EASTBOURNE, ENGLAND

NexGen® is an imprint of
Cook Communications Ministries, Colorado Springs, CO 80918
Cook Communications, Paris, Ontario
Kingsway Communications, Eastbourne, England

ONE REHEARSAL CHRISTMAS PLAYS
© 2004 by Cook Communications Ministries

First Printing, 2004
Printed in the United States of America
1 2 3 4 5 6 7 8 9 10 Printing/Year 08 07 06 05 04

Editorial Manager: Doug Schmidt
Product Developer: Karen Pickering
Design: Granite Design
Illustrations: Heiser Graphics

ISBN 0-7814-4120-X

Dedication

To Sue Samet, my dear friend, pianist, and co-director of skits and plays for over 20 years.

On a personal note . . .
For over a dozen years, my husband was the volunteer director of Christian Education at our small church. When it came time for the Christmas plays, he always looked to me for help. Because I love children, love the theater, and love Christmas, I actually found joy in that assignment. But I knew from the beginning, that as the mother of three active boys, I didn't want to spend hours and hours at the church rehearsing for the Christmas plays . . . hence the birth of ONE REHEARSAL CHRISTMAS PLAYS. Our goal was to glorify God, celebrate the birth of His son, and spend time on things other than memorizing parts for a 40-minute presentation one evening at church. Our goal was reached, and now I am pleased to share with you something that I hope will help you . . . glorify God, celebrate the birth of His Son, and give YOU time to focus on what is truly important during the holiday season and throughout the year! Merry Christmas!

Love and joy!
Kendra Smiley

Professional speaker and author of several books including her latest . . . *AARON'S WAY—The Journey of A Strong-Willed Child.*

Visit her at www.KendraSmiley.com

Table of Contents

Table of Contents

Basics for the Director

Here are some "helpful hints" to make your job as the director/producer go even more smoothly . . .

Speaking Parts:

Choose the more outgoing students for the parts requiring more talking. There are some parts that will require a small amount of memorization. Be sure to select actors that have no trouble with this task.

Don't demand that every line be memorized and spoken word for word. Instead, encourage the characters to deliver the essence of the message. There is an obvious exception if an important word or phrase is needed for the next speaker or if the actor is reciting a poem.

The speaking parts are very adaptable. They can be combined if you have fewer participants or divided into smaller parts to accommodate more students. (For example, a student can read four lines of a poem or only two. Two students can say a part together.) Your goal is to involve EVERYONE in one way or another. As students reach junior-high age, they typically prefer to be the nonspeaking nativity characters. By high school, they are usually ready to join in again with speaking and singing.

Photocopy and give the speaking parts to the students well in advance of your One Rehearsal. Encourage them to work with a parent or other adult to memorize them. Each Sunday school teacher may be responsible for the progress of this activity for the students in his/her class.

Look for a way to make the script available during the play to all the speaking characters without it being obtrusive. It will be a crutch rather than something to read. I have made suggestions in each play about "hiding the scripts."

Be very familiar with the play BEFORE the One Rehearsal. You, as the director, will need to help your characters understand the feeling and heart of the play. You may need to describe the attitude and demeanor of the various characters . . . grumpy, knowledgeable, silly, or whatever.

Music for the Play:

Teach the songs to the younger children long before the One Rehearsal. If the verses are complicated, have the older children sing those and the younger ones join in on the chorus each time. If you have children who are willing, the verses can even be solo parts . . . or phrases can be sung as solos.

The congregation loves to sing the Christmas songs. If you desire, they can join in on the singing. The easiest way to facilitate their involvement is to print the words and instructions in the bulletin. The pianist will be their director, leading with an introduction. If your music minister or song leader is available, that person can step in to lead at the appropriate time.

A pianist is extremely helpful. None of the songs are difficult, but if you have someone leading at the piano, it is much more effective. I suggest you begin every performance with a prelude of Christmas hymns and songs and conclude in a similar manner. If you are not familiar with the suggested songs, or if you cannot locate the music, you can substitute another song that is appropriate.

The Stage:

When I refer to the stage, I am referring to the pulpit area of your church. You can adapt stage direction to fit your setting. Also, you can create dramatic lighting if that is possible. In many smaller churches the options are usually all lights on or all lights off. If you have more options, use them.

There are some additional drawings of sets, stage decoration, and other suggestions to help make this program attractive, yet easy to plan and produce. Check for illustrations with each of the plays to see what kind of supplies or decorations can be used.

Opening and Closing the Program:

The pastor, or you as the director, can open with a welcome and prayer (after the prelude) and close with a hardy "Merry Christmas" (before the postlude) and perhaps an invitation to join together for cookies and punch at the conclusion of the play. Find some volunteers to spearhead the refreshment committee. (Many times, the director believes he or she can "do it all," and the event becomes too stressful.)

The idea is to involve the children in presenting a clear message of God's love as manifested by the birth of Jesus. The goal is not to showcase great talent or to spend an inordinate amount of time in preparation or performance. Giving children the opportunity to sing and speak before a crowd is something that will serve them well as they mature. It helps to build confidence, and the church setting is the perfect place to "test your wings" and find loving approval of your "performance."

The more relaxed and focused you are on "The Reason for the Season," the more that attitude and emphasis will permeate your group.

Costume Suggestions:

Costumes should be simple. It is always helpful if you have a committee who is responsible to find/create the costumes and the various props. They can also help the students get dressed for the performance.

Nativity Costumes:

All nativity costumes can be made from pieces of material (drab colors) that are 45" wide, folded with a neck opening cut into the center of the fold. Belts can be made from long scraps of material. Head pieces are also plain pieces of material gathered with a headband of material.

Angel Costumes:

Angels will need the same material pieces but in white. Haloes can be made of circles of tinsel garland placed on the angels' heads. Wings (if you choose to use them) can be purchased at novelty stores or ordered from costume catalogs.

Shepherd Costumes:

The clothing is the same as listed under Nativity Costumes. They need to wear the robe with the belt and the head piece. Shepherds staffs can be made of wrapping paper tubes fastened together with duct tape and then covered with "wooden-looking" self-adhesive paper.

If you save the costumes and props from year to year, adding a new item every so often, you will soon have a substantial collection for your Christmas plays.

Chapter 1

God's Gift to Us

Characters/Costumes:

- ❑ **Santa**—Santa suit
- ❑ **Adult shopper #1**—Outside clothing
- ❑ **Adult shopper #2**—Outside clothing
- ❑ **Carolers, all Sunday school Students**—Wearing coats, hats, scarves, and mittens
- ❑ **Mary**—Bible-time costume (See directions on page 9 in Basics for the Director.)
- ❑ **Joseph**—Bible-time costume (See directions on page 9 in Basics for the Director.)
- ❑ **Angel**—Angel costume (See directions on page 9 in Basics for the Director.)

Set Design and Props:

❏ **Sign**—"Your Town" Mall, surrounded with Christmas lights.

❏ **4 front doors**—made from refrigerator boxes or freezer paper.

❏ **Chair** for Santa.

❏ **Park bench**—for two weary shoppers.

❏ **Lots of packages**—for the two shoppers.

❏ **Jingle bells**

❏ **Doll/Baby Jesus**

❏ **Bible**

Setting:

Outside of a busy (and gaudy) shopping center . . . the (Name of Your Town) Mall. A sign marks the entrance to the mall, and Santa sits unassumingly in a chair in the back of the stage—"inside" the shopping mall. On the walls of the sanctuary are doors (nonfunctioning) made from large cardboard pieces or drawn on freezer paper and taped to the wall. Two weary shoppers enter and rest on a park bench sitting to the front, stage right, outside of the mall. They are loaded with packages and are very tired and a little disillusioned with the entire season. (Each shopper's lines can be taped on the back of a large shopping bag placed on her lap.)

The Play: God's Gift to Us

Shopper #1: *(Exhausted.)* Whew! I've had it with Christmas. I just spent over six hours inside that mall with everyone who lives in this town. If I see one more sprig of holly or hear another "Ho, ho, ho," from the *(Your Town)* Mall Santa, I think I may get sick!

Shopper #2: *(Nodding her head.)* I know what you mean. There was a lady in the men's clothing department who wanted to argue with the clerk about EVERYTHING!

Shopper #1: At least you FOUND a clerk. I finally gave up in housewares. *(Pause.)* This is all so exhausting! My feet hurt, my head hurts, my back hurts . . .

Shopper #2: *(Interrupting and holding up some packages.)* . . . and my credit card hurts!

(The carolers enter from the back of the church singing "Caroling, Caroling." The carolers go up to the stage area on stage left, outside the mall. When the song is finished, freeze action.)

Shopper #2: *(Rather disinterested.)* Nice music. Well, I guess not EVERYONE is in the mall. *(Gesturing toward the carolers.)* There's a group that isn't.

Shopper #1: Maybe they've already finished their shopping . . . or maybe they're smarter than we are, and they don't DO any!

Shopper #2: Who knows? All I know is that I could really use a holiday from this holiday!

(As soon as the word "holiday" is spoken, a caroler goes over to the first door and knocks. The carolers sing "Jingle Bells." Older students ring jingle bells on the chorus. At the conclusion of the song, all shout "Merry Christmas!" and freeze action.)

Shopper #1: *(Sighing and reminiscing a little.)* All that bell ringing reminds me of a chiming clock that my grandmother had in her dining room. *(Pause and then in a startled way.)* MY GRANDMOTHER!! Oh no, I forgot to get a gift for my grandmother. Is there still time? What time is it? It'll be midnight before I finish my shopping.

(As soon as the word "midnight" is spoken, a caroler goes over to the second door and knocks. The carolers sing "It Came Upon a Midnight Clear." At the close all shout "Merry Christmas!" and freeze action.)

Shopper #2: Did you hear what the carolers were singing? Christmas is a time of peace on earth. I usually feel like Christmas is a time of panic. There is so much to remember . . . you have to do the cards, and the cookies, and the decorating, and the programs, and the parties, and THE SHOPPING. *(By now she is completely exhausted!)* You may have forgotten your Grandmother, but I've been looking for over three days for the perfect gift for my mother.

Shopper #1: What kind of gift do you want to give her?

Shopper #2: I'm not exactly sure. It has to be beautiful and unusual and well, I don't know . . . just glorious!

(As soon as the word "glorious" is spoken, a caroler goes over to the third door and knocks. The carolers sing "Hark the Herald Angels Sing." At the close all shout "Merry Christmas!" and freeze action.)

Shopper #1: Those carolers are kind of cute. They seem to be having a good time.

Shopper #2: That's a lot more than I can say for the two of us. Maybe we're missing something.

Shopper #1: There must be more to this season than the hustle and bustle . . .

Shopper #2: . . . the baking and taking . . .

Shopper #1: . . . the meeting and eating . . .

Shopper #2: the SHOPPING AND DROPPING!!!

Both: There must be a better reason for this season!!!

(A caroler knocks on door 4, and they sing "Away in a Manger." The nativity characters enter as the singing begins. Mary, carrying baby Jesus/doll, Joseph, and the angel [carrying a Bible] enter together. At the conclusion of the song, carolers freeze and the Angel reads the Christmas story from Luke 2:1-14.)

Shopper #1: *(After the angel finishes.)* It must have been a wonderful night.

Shopper #2: Yes . . . a Silent Night . . . a Holy Night.

(The pianist plays a short introduction of "Silent Night" and all sing. Carolers draw close to the manger and look at the beautiful scene. As the song is being sung, Santa comes from the "Mall" and kneels at the manger.)

Shopper #1: I'm feeling a whole lot better than when we first sat down on this bench. Those carolers and their friends have helped me get an idea of what Christmas is REALLY all about.

Shopper #2: Me too!! It's not racing around to get the perfect gift . . .

Shopper #1: Or worrying about wrapping, delivering, or paying for that gift.

Shopper #2: Right! It's about Jesus. Jesus Christ, God's only Son, who came as a baby on that very first Christmas.

Shopper #1: *(More excited with each sentence.)* I wish that EVERYONE could understand what we just learned. I wish EVERYONE could hear those carolers. I wish EVERYONE could witness the real story from God's Word. I wish that EVERYONE could have a truly merry Christmas!

Shopper #2: Me too!!

"We Wish You a Merry Christmas" is sung by carolers and shoppers followed by shouting "Merry Christmas!"

The Party

Characters/Costumes:

- ❑ **Three groups of Sunday school students**—wearing normal everyday clothing
- ❑ **Carolers**—wearing coats, hats, scarves, and mittens
- ❑ **Mary**—Bible-time costume (See directions on page 9 in Basics for the Director.)
- ❑ **Joseph**—Bible-time costume (See directions on page 9 in Basics for the Director.)
- ❑ **Doll/Baby Jesus**—wrapped in a blanket
- ❑ **Angel**—Angel costume (See directions on page 9 in Basics for the Director.)

Set Design and Props:

- ❑ **Small undecorated tree**, in a tree stand
- ❑ **Ornaments for the tree**
- ❑ **Brightly wrapped presents**—big and small
- ❑ **Paper, ribbon, and other wrapping supplies**, including boxes, tape, scissors, etc.
- ❑ **Bibles**

Setting:

Kids are on the stage area. They are in small groups. One group is organizing Christmas ornaments, a second group is wrapping gifts, and the third group is searching the Scriptures. The pianist is playing Christmas tunes softly in the background. When she finishes, three students (one from each group) go to pulpit area. They can have their parts memorized or read them.

The Play: The Party

#1: Christmas is coming.
We're planning a party.
Come join us now.
We don't want to be tardy.

#2: You can help us get ready.
There's so much to do.
We want it just right
For Jesus and you.

#3: This party is special
Because, you will see,
It honors dear Jesus
A best friend to me.

(Each speaker goes back to a different small group. All the students on the stage sing "Happy Birthday, Jesus.")

(The next speaker comes to the front and center of the stage. He is from the "decorations" group. As he speaks, he picks up a small, undecorated tree that has been placed on the stage in advance.)

#4: First we put up decorations
Trim the tree so fine.
Silver bells and twinkling lights
Make our room just shine.

(All sing "Deck the Halls" including the older students singing off stage. As everyone sings, the speaker carries the small tree back to his group. The group puts ornaments on the tree.)

(The next speaker moves to the center of the stage. He's also from the "decorations" group. One or two students from this group need to move the decorated tree back to the designated spot on the stage.)

#5: What's that we heard outside this room?
It's carolers in song.
I love to hear the carols sung.
I'd listen all day long.

(All sing "Hark the Herald Angels Sing." As the singing begins, speaker #5 walks to the hall, a side door, or other entrance and opens the door for the carolers. They enter, leading the singing. At the conclusion of the song, the carolers divide up into the various groups of kids. They can remove their coats, hats, mittens, etc. and sit to one side if it's not distracting.)

(Student from the "wrapping" group goes to center stage carrying a gift.)

#6: Let's not forget the presents.
The gifts to one and all.
The packages are brightly wrapped.
Some great big and some small.

(The next speaker, also from the "wrapping" group, moves to the center of the stage carrying a gift.)

#7: **These presents are for others**
Whom we love and set apart.
The gift I give to Jesus
Is the gift within my heart.

(All sing "It Came Upon a Midnight Clear" as "wrapping" group goes to the little tree and put their gifts under it.)

(A student from the "Scripture" group moves to center stage with a Bible.)

#8: **There is one more important thing**
We want to emphasize.
The Bible tells about the birth.
It's right before our eyes.

(All sing "Away in a Manger" as student carries the Bible to the altar and the nativity characters enter and freeze action at center stage. At the conclusion of the song the angel reads Luke 2:1-14.)

All sing "Silent Night."

(The final speaker comes to center stage.)

#9: **Our Christmas can be merry**
And filled with cheer and joy.
All because of Jesus
God's precious little boy!

(All sing "We Wish You a Merry Christmas!")

'Twas the Night Before Christmas

Characters/Costumes:

- ❑ **Two Readers**
- ❑ **Mr. Mouse**—mouse ears, nose, and tail (if possible)
- ❑ **Angels**—Angel costume (See directions on page 9 in Basics for the Director.)
- ❑ **Little Angel**—Angel costume (See directions on page 9 in Basics for the Director.)
- ❑ **Gabriel the Angel**—Angel costume (See directions on page 9 in Basics for the Director.)
- ❑ **Innkeeper**—Bible-time costume (See directions on page 9 in Basics for the Director.)
- ❑ **Shepherds**—Bible-time costume (See directions on page 9 in Basics for the Director.)
- ❑ **Mary**—Bible-time costume (See directions on page 9 in Basics for the Director.)
- ❑ **Joseph**—Bible-time costume (See directions on page 9 in Basics for the Director.)

Set Design and Props:

- ❑ **Two stools for readers**
- ❑ **Large book** made from poster board with the title *'Twas the Night Before Christmas*
- ❑ **Large book** made from poster board with the title *'Twas the Night Before Christ's Birth*

- ❏ **Apron, large bowl, and spoon** for Mr. Mouse
- ❏ **Heavenly Host Classics songbooks for angels** (Can be books covered with white paper with the title written on it.)
- ❏ **Scroll for Gabriel** (Can be made from roll of drawing paper, etc.)
- ❏ **Broom for innkeeper**
- ❏ **"List of Things to Do"** for innkeeper (Written on large paper. The title should be large enough for the audience to see and read. The Innkeeper's lines can be attached to this list so only the Innkeeper can read them.)

Setting:

There are two stools set close together on the pulpit/stage area. The Readers sit on these stools and pick up one big book entitled *'Twas the Night Before Christmas*. Mr. Mouse is to the side with his back turned. The Readers read their lines from the books and Mr. Mouse can have his lines inside the big bowl. The books are very large with the titles clearly visible.

The Play: 'Twas the Night Before Christmas

Reader #1: *(Reading from 'Twas the Night Before Christmas.)*
'Twas the night before Christmas
And all through the house
Not a creature was stirring
Not even a mouse.

Mouse: *(Turns around, wearing apron and holding large bowl and spoon and stirring wildly. He speaks in an irritated manner.)* Hold it a minute. That was your first mistake. I'm stirring like crazy to get these Christmas goodies finished. There is no rest for this hard-workin' mouse. *(He turns back around in a huff.)*

Reader #2: *(Attention shifts back to their reading.)*
The stockings were hung
By the chimney with care
In hopes that St. Nicholas
Soon would be there.

Mouse: *(Turning face forward again.)* Oops! That's mistake number two. Those socks are by the fireplace to dry out. The kids in this house can't seem to stay out of the wet snow!! *(Stays facing forward as he listens to the readers.)*

Reader #1: *(Reading.)*
The children were nestled
All snug in their beds
While visions of sugar plums
Danced in their heads.

Mouse: *(Disgustedly.)* Sugar plums, smurgar plums!! These kids are dreaming about gifts!! Gifts and stuff and things!! They don't care if the stuff dances or not. They just like the loot.

Reader #2: *(Turns to the mouse.)* Mr. Mouse, you certainly seem negative. Are you a little disturbed by Christmas?

Mouse: Christmas. Bah, humbug. All it is is work and worry and loot and bills and gimme, gimme, gimme, got it!

Reader #1: Oh no, Mr. Mouse. Christmas is MUCH, MUCH more than that. Let me grab the 1st edition of *The Night Before Christmas* and see if that will help you understand. *(Reader #1 gets the second big book, 'Twas the Night Before Christ's Birth and sits down again, sharing the book with Reader #2.)* Now settle down and listen.

Reader #2: *(Reading.)*
'Twas the night before Christ's birth
And up in the sky
The angels were prepping
To be "heard on high."

(Angels come on to stage area adjusting their gowns and wings and checking their halos. They have songbooks, Heavenly Host Classics, which can conceal their lines. Gabriel has a scroll containing his lines.)

Angel #1: *(Excitedly.)* Tonight's the night! God is sending Jesus down to earth.

Angel #2: *(Speaking to Gabriel.)* I'm so excited! Who should we tell the news to first?

Gabriel: Let me look at our assignment scroll. *(Reading from the scroll.)* We are to go to the hills outside of Bethlehem to a group of shepherds.

Angel #2: Shepherds? Shouldn't we tell some important people?

Reader #1: *(Obviously eavesdropping, he interrupts the angels.)* It's God's plan for you to tell the shepherds first. The birth is just the beginning of the plan.

Angel #1: Well, God knows best. Let's get the other angels and head out. Lead on, Gabriel.

(Gabriel leads the angels to stage left where they pick up the little angels and walk toward center stage with both readers and Mr. Mouse to stage right. Angels lead the congregation in singing "Away in a Manger," then exit.)

Reader #1: *(Reading.)*
The people in Bethlehem
A small rural town
Were just getting ready
To lay themselves down.

(Innkeeper enters with his broom sprucing things up. He comes down the center aisle and speaks as he approaches the front. He has a "List of Things to Do" under his arm and refers to it as he speaks. This list can contain his lines.)

Innkeeper: *(Hurriedly.)* I have so much to do! I have never seen so many people in town! This tax census from the Romans is really causing a lot of headaches. My place is so full, I've had to turn people away. Just a little while ago, a young couple begged me to let them stay in my stable. *(Pause.)* I let them. The wife is expecting a baby any time now. *(Pause, sighing deeply.)* I suppose it IS better than sleeping in the street. *(Looks offstage left.)* Maybe I should check on that couple. No, they'll be alright. *(He sweeps his way back out the aisle.)*

(As the Innkeeper exits, the shepherds enter and take their positions. The shepherds recline as though preparing to sleep.)

Reader #2: *(Reading.)*
And out on the hillside
While watching their sheep
A group of young shepherds
Were falling asleep.
When suddenly out of the sky
Came a light *[additional light is turned on if possible]*
An angel appeared
Making everything bright!

Gabriel: *(Enters with other angels and addresses the shepherds.)*
Peace to each man!
You need not have fear
For the news we have brought
You will find very dear.

Angel #1: A baby is born
This night is His birth.
He's come to save all
Of the people on earth.

Angel #2: In Bethlehem town
You will find this dear child
With Joseph and Mary,
His mother so mild.

Angel #1: Sharing a manger
With oxen and sheep
Nestled in blankets
The babe, sound asleep.

Angel #2: Good news we bring
you this wonderful night.

Little Angel: *(Interrupting.)* Jesus is born!!

Angel #2: Let us run to the site.

(All sing "Angels We Have Heard on High." Angels exit and shepherds reflect on this amazing message.)

Shepherd #1: A vision!

Shepherd #2: Did you hear what the angels said? Jesus is born!

Shepherd #3: We must do what the angels told us to do! Let's go and look for the stable.

Shepherd #1: The Lord will take care of the sheep. Let's hurry!

(All shepherds exit. Mary, Joseph, and the baby enter and take their positions on the pulpit/stage area as music plays softly. The action freezes.)

Reader #1: *(Reading.)*
So after the angels
Delivered the news
The shepherds went searching
With no time to lose.
And just as the angels
Had told them aloud,
They found Jesus with Mary
And Joseph, so proud.

Reader #2: Reads Luke 2:1-14 *(Soft music plays in the background—"Silent Night.")*

(At the conclusion of reading all sing "Silent Night.")

Mouse: Wow! That's a great story! Jesus was born on that first Christmas Day?

Reader #2: *(Reading.)*
That's right!
Jesus was born
On the first Christmas Day.
A gift from the Father…
He planned it that way.

Reader #1: *(Reading.)*
And every dear person
Who hears and believes
That moment from Jesus
A pardon receives.
For all folks have sinned
And have gone their own way
But God listens closely
When we choose to pray.

And choose to love Jesus
Who came down to earth
To live and to die
And to give us new birth.

Mouse: *(Excitedly.)* Terrific!! Christmas isn't all loot and
gimme, gimme, gimme, got to! It's really Jesus
and joy and love straight from God.

Reader #2: Congratulations! Now you know the reason
for the season.

(All sing "Joy to the World.")

Chapter 4

Wild West Christmas

Characters/Costumes

- ☐ **Mary**—Bible-time costume (See directions on page 9 in Basics for the Director.)
- ☐ **Joseph**—Bible-time costume (See directions on page 9 in Basics for the Director.)
- ☐ **Jesus**—Bible-time costume (See directions on page 9 in Basics for the Director.)
- ☐ **Angels**—Angel costume (See directions on page 9 in Basics for the Director.)
- ☐ **Shepherds**—Bible-time costume (See directions on page 10 in Basics for the Director.)
- ☐ **Doc**—Western clothing and hat
- ☐ **Wild Bill Hiccup**—Western clothing
- ☐ **Claire**—Western clothing
- ☐ **Baby/young toddler**
- ☐ **Singers**

Set Design and Props:

- ❑ **Barrel or bench**
- ❑ **Diary**
- ❑ **Invitation**—very crumpled
- ❑ **Blanket**
- ❑ **Maps**
- ❑ **Small doll**—Jesus

Setting:

A "live" nativity is "frozen" on the center stage. Mary, Joseph, baby Jesus, angel, and shepherds are part of this scene. At the conclusion of the prelude there is a ruckus offstage.

The Play: Wild West Christmas

Doc: *(Reading offstage.)* Whoa girl! Steady now—that's a girl! Good horse. Nice Daisybelle! I'll just turn you out here to graze in the church yard. *(Enters, removes his hat, and dusts himself off. His script is inside his hat.)* Whew, what a ride! That Daisybelle is sure frisky! *(Looking around.)* Things look mighty nice in here! It's good to be in *[Your Town].* *(Doc sits on barrel or bench and writes in his diary. His script can now be in the diary.)*

Doc: Dear Diary—Welp! I finally made it to *[Your Town]* . . . mighty nice place! I sure was tickled to git this here invitation *(Holds it up for audience to see.)* from the Preacher. *(Quits writing and addresses the crowd.)* Look at this here thing. It's been through a lot! Why it was postmarked on August 30 and delivered on December 12! Preacher said the church was fixin' to have a Christmas program here and that me and Wild Bill Hiccup and Claire, the Calamity Kid, was all invited. Yahoo! It tweren't easy gitttin' here—had to wrassle a pole cat in *[a town near yours]* and got jumped by a varmit in *[another nearby town].* But, we're here now . . . or should I say I'm here now. I'll be dadgummed if'n I know where Wild Bill and Claire are! Well, *(Back to writing in the diary.)* Dear Diary, I'm signing off for now. I'm agonna snuggle up with this here blanket and wait for the fun to begin. I'm also gonna watch for Wild Bill and Claire. *(He lies down near the stage with his blanket.)*

(Pianist plays "Come on Ring Those Bells" and Sunday school kids go to the stage area and sing. When finished they return to their seats.)

(After the song Wild Bill and Claire enter from the back of the church, looking over their maps. Their scripts are on the maps.)

Bill: Shooey! I ain't heared such purty singin' in a long time. *(Looking around.)* Look! Here's some boys and girls and some older folks too. I telled you, Claire, we gist had to follow the sound of that purty music.

Claire: *(Waving.)* Hi guys and gals! Thanks for the invite to your program! We finally made it! *(Looking around.)* Why look there! *(She gestures toward the nativity scene on the stage.)* Did you kids see that?

Bill: Why shore they saw it! They'd have to have their eyes closed to miss it. *(He studies the scene for a minute.)* It is mighty fine except fer one thing.

Claire: What's that??!!

Bill: It's missin' my favorite nativity animal. Where's the buffalo?

Claire: Buffalo? There twern't no buffalo in Bethlehem. Where'd you git thet silly notion?

Bill: From my favoritest Christmas carol.

Claire: Huh?

Bill: *(Singing words to tune of "Home on the Range.")* Oh give me a nest where the buffalo rest, and there's lights and an angel on top.

Claire: Oh brother! Well, thet there scene has my favorite part. *(Acting shy.)* I'm kinda partial to shepherds. I think they're really cute guys!

Bill: Aren't you thinkin' about the wisemen? They're cute guys, and wise guys!!

Claire: Humph! *(Ignoring him . . . pause.)* Anyway, I like the Baby Jesus too! Babies are soooooooooooo adorable!!

Bill: Babies??? Baby Jesus?? What in tarnation are you jaw-in'about? There aren't no babies in that there nativity scene.

Claire: Oh yes there is. There's one!

Bill: Why would there be a baby?

Claire: 'Cause Jesus started out that way!

Bill: *(Arguing.)* Did not!

Claire: Did too!

Bill: Why would God do that? Babies ain't good for nothing. All they do is eat and wet and spit up. And all that stuff stinks! I can't hardly stand babies.

Claire: *(Knowingly.)* Well, Jesus started thet there way. God knew that baby Jesus could make a difference!

(By now Claire and Bill are down front and have joined Doc.)

Doc: Howdy Wild Bill! Howdy Calamity Claire!

Both: Howdy Doc!

Doc: Where you been? The program done already got started.

Claire: Well, we were lost! And Bill wouldn't ask fer directions. *(Shakes her map.)*

Bill: *(Grandly.)* We weren't lost. Maybe jest a bit confused. But the important thing is we're here now! Let the program begin.

Doc: It did already!

Bill: Oh . . . well . . . let's sit down and watch it.

(As the pianist plays "Away in a Manger," the Sunday school kids go up to the pulpit area. They sing "Away in a Manger" then exit.)

Bill: *(Enthusiastically.)* Whoa ned! That was powerful good! You kids are good singers! Me too! *(Singing.)* "Oh give me a nest, where the buffalo rest . . . "

Claire: *(Puts her hand over Bill's mouth.)* Whoa, Wild Bill. That's enough! Your singing is getting' better and better, but don't you go and over-practice now.

Bill: Thanks, Calamity! I'm still confused, though. What is all this "baby" stuff? The kids was singin' about it too. How can a baby preach or teach or heal—or die on a cross?

Claire: *(Hushing him.)* Shhh! Here comes somebody else. Maybe you'll have an answer soon.

(Soloist sings "One Small Child.")

Bill: *(To soloist.)* Good job. You keep practicing and you'll git as good as me! No braggin' intended. *(He hesitates, scratches his head, and then continues.)* I still don't get that baby stuff though. Oh well. *(Pauses.)* Hey, did any of you folks notice that while that solo was being sung there was a GREAT BIG . . . RAT running across the floor? *(Very excited.)* Ladies, put your feet up. I will save you. *(Stomps on the floor with his boots.)* Never fear, Bill is here! *(He exits and reenters carrying an older baby . . . at arms' length.)* That tweren't a rat!! That was this here baby. He was crawling across that there floor! *(Speaks to baby.)* Shame on you! Oh . . . he smiled at me. Did you kids see that? This here baby smiled at me! Cootchey, cootchey, coo! *(Sniffs baby.)* Why THIS baby don't stink. *(Smells himself.)* I do, jest a little. *(Laughs.)* But, this here baby smells good. Why, I think this baby likes me. *(Pauses.)* Shucks. I think I like this here baby!

(The pianist plays "Silent Night," and the angel reads Luke 2:1–14. Bill and the baby listen to the Scripture. The background music plays until the angel is finished.)

Bill: *(Thoughtfully.)* I think that I'm beginning to git the big picture . . . *(Looking at baby.)* or should I say the little picture. Jesus started as a little baby so that he'd really know how I feel when I'm tired or sad or when I'm tempted. This here baby *(Looks at the baby.)* . . . why he'll know what it feels like to be a man some day. It all makes sense. What a good plan! By golly, when God does it, He does it right!!

All sing "Joy to the World."

Bill: *(At the completion of the hymn.)* Thanks again for invitin' us! This here was the best Christmas program I done ever seen or heard.

Doc and Claire: *(Together.)* Me too! Ya'll have a very merry Christmas, ya hear? *(Bill hands the baby to someone and Bill, Doc, and Claire exit.)*

The Christmas Story

Jesus Christ Is the Same— Yesterday, Today, and Forever!

Characters/Costumes

- ❑ **Boy**—winter coat
- ❑ **Girl**—winter coat
- ❑ **Angel**—Angel costume (See directions on page 9 in Basics for the Director.)
- ❑ **Shepherds**—Bible-time costume (See directions on page 10 in Basics for the Director.)
- ❑ **Modern-day shepherds**—business man, homemaker, farmer, secretary, pastor, teacher, retired person, student, waitress, accountant
- ❑ **Wise men**—Bible-time costume (See directions on page 9 in Basics for the Director.)
- ❑ **Modern-day wise men**—Normal attire
- ❑ **Mary**—Bible-time costume (See directions on page 9 in Basics for the Director.)
- ❑ **Joseph**—Bible-time costume (See directions on page 9 in Basics for the Director.)
- ❑ **Jesus**—Bible-time costume (See directions on page 9 in Basics for the Director.)

Set Design/Props:

- ❑ **Book**
- ❑ **Magazine**
- ❑ **Two chairs**
- ❑ **Manger**
- ❑ **Bible**
- ❑ **Shepherds' staffs**

❑ **Briefcase, bowl and spoon, hat, steno pad and pen, Bible, pointer or yardstick, AARP sticker and tour brochure, backpack, apron and tray, calculator**—for the modern shepherds

❑ **Gold, frankincense and myrrh**—wisemen (jewelry boxes)

❑ **Cookies**

❑ **Clothes** (For the rescue mission.)

❑ **Collection plate**

Setting:

Outside the church. Two kids meet each other at the center of the stage—one comes from stage left, one comes from stage right. They literally bump into each other. One is engrossed in reading a book, and the other is looking at a magazine. (Scripts are hidden in the book and the magazine.) Neither is paying attention to where he or she is going.

The Play: The Christmas Story

Boy: *(Startled!)* Oops! Sorry. I wasn't paying attention. Hi! What's new with you?

Girl: *(Equally surprised.)* I wasn't paying attention either. Sorry. Not much new with me . . . what's new with you?

Boy: Oh, I'm on my way to our church's Christmas program. Hey, do you want to come along? The church is just around the corner. It'll be great! Come on. You'll really like it. It's always a great program!

Girl: *(Hesitating.)* Awwwww—I don't know. I'm kind of busy. Anyway, if you ask me, it sounds like a bore. I've heard the Christmas story before—Mary, Joseph, the baby—shepherds, angels, wise men. It's kind of like watching a rerun on T.V. And besides, what in the world does any of that have to do with today? After all—all that stuff happened over 2000 years ago. Things change, you know.

Boy: You might be surprised! In the Bible there is a verse that says that Jesus is the same "yesterday, today and forever!" He never changes. I think that you just might learn a thing or two from that old, old story.

(Pianist plays "Victory in Jesus" softly and then louder.)

Boy: Come on—I hear the music coming from the church. Let's go to the program, and when it's over we'll get a milkshake.

Girl: Oh . . . alright. But if this is as boring as a T.V. rerun, YOU'RE buying the shake—and I like chocolate!!

Boy: Don't worry . . . Let's go!

(Both exit, and come in the front door of the church. As they exit, the pianist begins to play Christmas music.)

All sing "Joy to the World" and "O Little Town of Bethlehem."

Boy and girl come in as the singing begins, and go to two chairs on far stage right and remove their coats. As the congregation sings "O Little Town of Bethlehem," the manger scene actors move to their places . . . Mary, Joseph, the baby, and the Christmas angel.

Girl: *(After the singing is complete, speaks in a loud whisper.)* Here we go with the rerun. It's like reading old comics.

Boy: Shhhhhhhhhhhh—the angel is speaking.

Angel reads from the Bible—Luke 2:1-14.

Boy: Those angels were praising God. People still praise the Lord today.

(The youngest Sunday school kids go up to the stage. They sing "Away in a Manger." When they finish, they exit.)

Girl: Those little kids were pretty good. They did make a joyful noise. I guess that IS praising the Lord. Okay, that part is the same.

Boy: You bet it is! We do it all the time around here. Shhh . . . here goes the angel again.

Angel reads again from Luke 2:15-16 (Halfway through verse 15, the shepherds enter down the aisle and walk slowly toward the manger.)

Girl: Now tell me what the shepherds have to do with [current year]!! I know there are still people who raise sheep, but they don't dress like that or run around with those big sticks.

Boy: True, we don't have shepherds like that today. But herding sheep was a very popular job back then. Today we have other jobs we do. Here come some modern-day shepherds. (Students enter. They assume poses.)

Girl: Huh? I don't get it.

Boy: These people all have jobs that they do each day. (Each Modern-Day Shepherd steps forward as "introduced.") See, there's a business man (carrying briefcase), a homemaker (with a bowl and spoon), a farmer (wearing a hat), a secretary (holding a steno pad and pen), a pastor (with his Bible), a teacher (carrying a pointer), a retired person (with an AARP sticker and tour brochure), a student (wearing a backpack), a waitress (wearing an apron and balancing a tray), and an accountant (with a calculator).

They have jobs just like the shepherds had sheep, but the sheep or those jobs don't have to be the most important things in their lives. Jesus wants to be #1!

Girl: You mean that even though they all have work to do, Jesus still comes first for them? You mean that if God gave them a job to do they'd leave their tractors and desks to serve Him . . . just like the shepherds left their sheep?

Boy: That's right!! It's still the same! *(Modern shepherds exit.)*

Girl: I think I'm beginning to get the picture. Oh, listen . . . there's more.

Angel reads from the Matthew 2:1-11 (At the appropriate time the angel is reading in verse 1, the wise men enter and move toward the manger.)

Girl: I'm sure I already know the answer to this question, but here goes. Are there still wise men today?

Boy: Yes . . . in a sense. There are still many gifts we can bring to Jesus just like those kings from the East. People today still bring gifts to Jesus. *(Modern-Day Wise Men enter and step forward as they are "introduced.")* See, that boy is bringing some cookies. They are probably for the love boxes. And that girl is carrying clothes that will be sent to the rescue mission, and that boy is putting money in the collection plate. *(They exit.)*

Girl: Boy, I've really learned a thing or two this evening. Even though the Christmas Story first happened over 2000 years ago, it is still alive today. JESUS is alive today! He really is the same yesterday, today, and forever.

Boy: That's right!!! Well, should we go for that milkshake now? Looks like it's dutch treat—you buy your own!

(Music plays and kids all go on stage.)

(Boy and girl stand and then notice the kids on stage.)

Girl: But wait. The kids are going up on the stage again. Maybe they have another song. I want to stay and listen. All that I've learned tonight is going to make this the best Christmas yet—a very merry Christmas! *(Both sit back down.)*

Music: (The pianist plays an introduction, and all on stage sing "We Wish You a Merry Christmas!")

ALL: MERRY CHRISTMAS!!!

Chapter 6

Deck the Halls and Trim the Tree

Characters/Costumes:

- ❏ **Carolers**—outdoor clothing (This can be all the children in your Sunday school.)
- ❏ **Liz**—one of the carolers (An older child.)
- ❏ **Danny**—one of the carolers (An older child.)
- ❏ **Ben**—one of the carolers (An older child.)
- ❏ **Sue**—one of the carolers (An older child.)
- ❏ **Jason**—one of the carolers (An older child.)
- ❏ **Mary**—Bible-time costume (See directions on page 9 in Basics for the Director.)
- ❏ **Joseph**—Bible-time costume (See directions on page 9 in Basics for the Director.)
- ❏ **Jesus (doll or infant)**—wrapped in a blanket
- ❏ **Angels**—Angel costume (See directions on page 9 in Basics for the Director.)
- ❏ **Shepherds**—Bible-time costume (See directions on page 10 in Basics for the Director.)

Set Design and Props:

- ❏ **Caroling books**
- ❏ **Undecorated tree with lights in a tree stand**
- ❏ **Decoration box**
- ❏ **Ornaments**—bells, angel, shiny star
- ❏ **Doll**

Setting:

There is an undecorated tree in the middle of the stage. (It does have lights on it, but they are unlit.) The carolers enter singing "Deck the Halls." They move to the stage, sit down, and take off their coats. All the lines are written in the "caroling" books.

The Play: Deck the Halls and Trim the Tree

Liz: (Standing up.) Caroling was lots of fun! We went to the nursing home and to see [people in your church].

Danny: (Standing and interrupting.) And to _____ [Name of people in your church.] and to _____ [People in your church.].

All Carolers: (Standing and interrupting.) And ALL over _____ [Name of your town.]!

Ben: That really WAS fun, but decorating this tree looks like WORK. I need a rest (He plops down again.).

All Carolers: (Encouraging Ben.) Come on, you don't need a rest.

Liz: (Tugging at Ben.) It won't be toooo bad. You'll perk up after we start the job.

Danny: I know what will help. Let's sing a song.

All Carolers: Yeah! Yeah! (All agree but Ben remains seated.)

(Carolers sing "Come on Ring Those Bells." On the word "rest" they all point to Ben who then rises and joins in.).

Sue: (Excitedly.) That was great. Let's get started!

Jason: I'm ready!! (He peers inside a big box.) There's lots of stuff in this decorations box.

Sue: *(Nudging him aside.)* Let me see. Wow!

Jason: Where did they get the idea for all these great decorations? *(All carolers sit, and older kids with speaking parts go to the center stage when it is their turn to recite.)*

Liz: We're going to trim the Christmas tree,
And as we do you're going to see,
It points the way to God above,
It tells of Jesus and His love.
(Liz sits after recitation.)

(All Carolers stand together and sing "Come, Thou Long-Expected Jesus.")

Danny: *(Walks to center stage and pulls bells out of the decoration box.)*
The bells rang out a message
Of a manger filled with hay
Where God's Son, Baby Jesus
Was born on Christmas Day.
(He puts a bell on the tree and sits with the carolers again.)

(All carolers stand and sing "Away in a Manger.")

Sue: *(Pulls an angel out of the decorations box.)*
The angels' happy voices
Sang of "good will here on earth."
They told the shepherds in the field,
Of the dear Savior's birth.

(Sue puts the angel on the tree as all the rest of the carolers sing "Angels We Have Heard on High.")

Jason: *(Gets a star from the decorations box and moves to center stage.)*
God placed a bright and shining star
To guide the wise men on their way
Across the desert and the hills
To find the place where Jesus lay.
(Jason puts the star on the tree, and someone plugs in the Christmas tree lights as all carolers sing "We Three Kings.")

Liz: Great Job!! The tree looks beautiful.

Danny: *(Enthusiastically.)* And it really wasn't too much work. *(Looking at Ben.)* Was it?

Ben: *(Reluctantly.)* I guess not. It does look good.

Sue: (Walks over to the decorations box and looks inside.) Wait! There's still something in the decorations box.

Jason: (Joins Sue and looks inside the box with astonishment.) It's a baby doll.

Liz: (Unbelieving.) A baby?

Danny: Why is there a baby in the box? In the Christmas box?

All carolers sing "What Child Is This?" as the nativity actors take their places on the stage and freeze into position. At the conclusion of the song, the angel reads Luke 2:1-14.

Danny: Oh, I see.

Liz: Me, too. This baby doll represents Jesus. He is no decoration. He is the reason that we decorate and celebrate—THE REASON FOR THE SEASON!

All carolers stand together sing "Silent Night" followed by "We Wish You a Merry Christmas!"

Chapter 7

The Good News Flash

Characters/Costumes:

- ❑ **Editor-in-chief**—dressed professionally
- ❑ **Fred, Joyce, and Connie**—dressed like reporters, with press cards in their hats (trench coat, etc.)
- ❑ **Shepherds 1, 2, and 3**—Shepherd costumes (See directions on page 10 in Basics for the Director.)
- ❑ **Innkeeper**—Bible-time costume (See directions on page 9 in Basics for the Director.)
- ❑ **Mary**—Bible-time costume (See directions on page 9 in Basics for the Director.)
- ❑ **Joseph**—Bible-time costume (See directions on page 9 in Basics for the Director.)
- ❑ **Angel**—angel costume (See directions on page 9 in Basics for the Director.)
- ❑ **Singers**

Set Design/Props:

- ❑ **Desk** (in-out basket, desk light, laptop computer, etc.) **and chair**
- ❑ **Wastebasket**—filled to overflowing
- ❑ **Notepads and pens for 3 reporters**
- ❑ **3 hats with press cards**
- ❑ **Sheep herders' log book**
- ❑ **Fake doors made from freezer paper (optional)**

- ❑ **"NO VACANCY" signs**—(one has Christmas lights around the perimeter)
- ❑ **Newspaper**
- ❑ **Manger**
- ❑ **Shepherds' Staffs**—Shepherd costumes (See directions on page 10 in Basics for the Director.)

Note in Bulletin:

We have combined the past and the present. Use your imagination . . . for although the times have changed, Jesus Christ is present and is the same "yesterday, today, and forever."

Setting:

There is a desk and chair and a wastebasket that is overflowing. On the desk is a crowded in-out basket, a desk light, and laptop computer. There is a sign on the front of the desk which reads . . . EDITOR-IN-CHIEF, BETHLEHEM TIMES. On the wall is a very large calendar reading . . . TODAY IS December 26, 0000.

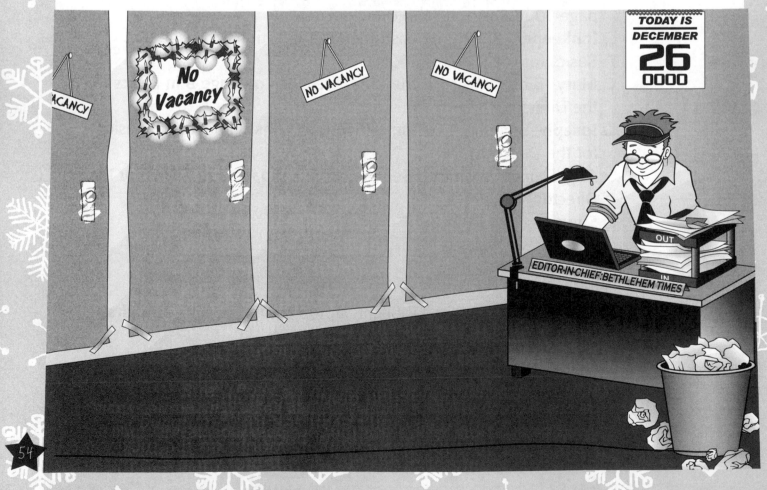

The Play: The Good News Flash

CHIEF: The Chief is seated at his desk. His lines are among the many papers on his desk. *(Excitedly.)* Fred, Joyce, Connie!! Come in here! There's a story breaking. I can feel it in my bones!!

(Reporters Fred, Joyce, and Connie saunter in with notepads in hand. Their lines are on the pads.)

FRED: *(Disinterested.)* Sure there's a story . . . Bethlehem is packed to overflowing with the ancestors of David coming here to pay taxes and be counted.

CONNIE: *(Joining in.)* Yeah! The roadways are congested—donkeys, camels, walkers . . . it's tough to find a parking spot!

JOYCE: *(Disgusted.)* That's not all that's tough to find . . . I saw NO VACANCY signs in every Inn window. Whew! I'm glad I'm a permanent resident of Bethlehem and not a traveler. I'll bet some folks are going to find themselves out in the cold. *(Knowingly.)* They'll wish they had called for a reservation.

CHIEF: *(Still excited.)* No, no . . . that's not what I'm talking about. Sure, that's big news, but I'm convinced there's REALLY big news out there. I've just got a hunch—and *(Pointing to Fred, Joyce, and Connie.)* you're going to see if my hunch is correct. Now get going!!

FRED: But where?

CHIEF: EVERYWHERE!! Fred, you go out to the fields and ask the shepherds if they've seen anything funny or unusual in the last 24 hours. Joyce, you go to the local inns—interview the innkeepers. They are always up on the latest events. Clare, you start poking around town. Check the houses and the marketplace and the stables. Talk to some of the strangers in town. And do it NOW!! *(They hurriedly exit stage right.) (To himself.)* My hunches usually pan out. I feel like there's a story out there and I want to see it on Page One of the BETHLEHEM TIMES . . . BEFORE I see it in the *Tribune*!!

(The Chief exits stage right. The shepherds enter stage left and get settled. Fred enters from stage right wearing a trench coat and hat with a PRESS card stuck in the front. He carries a steno pad and pencil. His lines can be on that pad for easy reference.)

FRED: Man, I always get the agri-business assignments. "Check with the shepherds." What good will that do? We all know that they were busy "watching over their flocks by night."

(The shepherds and Fred "freeze" in position as the younger elementary kids go to stage and sing "The First Noel" verses 1 and 2. After the song, the singers return to their seats.)

FRED: *(Shouting to the shepherds.)* Hey you. Yeah, you!! I'm Fred from the BETHLEHEM TIMES, and I wondered if I could ask you a few questions. *(The shepherds are obviously startled.)* Hey, don't be afraid.

SHEPHERD 1: *(Sarcastically.)* That's not the first time we've heard THAT in the last 24 hours.

FRED: *(Questioning.)* What do you mean?

SHEPHERD 2: You won't believe what happened last night!

FRED: Sure I will . . . try me.

SHEPHERD 3: Well, we were out here watching over our flocks by night . . .

FRED: *(Interrupting.)* That figures.

SHEPHERD 3: . . . when an angel of the Lord appeared to us and the glory of the Lord was shining all around us and we were really afraid.

FRED: You're kidding???

SHEPHERD 2: *(To audience.)* See, I told you he wouldn't believe it.

FRED: No, no, go on . . . please. I want to get this all down. *(Writing frantically.)*

SHEPHERD 3: Well, I wrote it all down in my sheep herders' log book so that I wouldn't forget . . . anyway, we were afraid, and then the angel said that a Savior who is Christ the Lord is born in the city of David. The angel said we would find the baby wrapped up and lying in a manger. And then, all of a sudden, there were so many angels who were praising and giving glory to God. *[NOTE: You can also have the shepherd quote directly from Luke 2:9-14.]*

FRED: *(To himself.)* WOW! The Chief was right. *(To shepherds.)* Did you go to the manger? Can you take me?

SHEPHERD 2: *(To Fred.)* We had a star to guide us, but I think I can remember the way. I'll take him. *(To the other shepherds.)* You guys watch the sheep.

(The shepherds, sheep, and Fred exit. Connie enters dressed just like Fred, and goes from door to door. You can either make door fronts from freezer paper, or Connie can just pantomime knocking on each door. It is obvious that she is obtaining no information, and she is getting disgusted with her pursuit.)

CONNIE: *(Disgusted.)* "Street detail." All I ever get is "street detail." This door-to-door stuff is for the birds. *(She knocks on the next door and again gets no information.)*

(Connie exits. "NO VACANCY" signs are placed on each door or on the wall if you have chosen not to make door. One of the "NO VACANCY" has blinking Christmas lights around the perimeter. When that sign is plugged in, Joyce enters.)

JOYCE: *(Dressed like Fred and Connie, stops and takes off her shoe and rubs her foot.)* Boy, I didn't realize that there were so many inns in Bethlehem—and all of them are full. So far I'm drawing a big ZERO. Well, here's my last one. It looks pretty full too!! I'll see if THIS innkeeper knows anything. *(The action "freezes.")*

(Younger elementary kids go to stage and sing "Away in a Manger." After the song, the singers return to their seats.)

JOYCE: *(Knocks on the door and the Innkeeper appears with a newspaper in hand.)* Uh, sir, excuse me . . .

INNKEEPER: *(In a hurried manner. His script is in his news-paper.)* No room. No room. I tell you, there's no room!! Didn't you see the NO VACANCY sign in the window? The salesman told me that the flashing lights would do the trick . . . but YOU didn't even see it!! *(Grumbling.)* Twenty denari down the drain!!

JOYCE: *(Flustered.)* Yes sir, no sir, I mean I DID see your sign. I'm not looking for a room. I'm from the *BETHLEHEM TIMES* and I want to ask you a few questions.

INNKEEPER: *(MUCH more pleasant attitude.)* Oh, really? *(Arranging his hair.)* Did you bring a photographer? *(Looks over her shoulder for the cameraman.)* Are you running an article on quality inns? Would you like my picture by the mantle or at the registration desk?

JOYCE: I just wondered if you noticed anything last night . . . anything unusual?

INNKEEPER: *(Thinking.)* Well, now that you mention it, last night was not your typical evening. There were so many people in Bethlehem. Why, I was turning them away right and left . . . telling them "next time call for a reservation." *(Joyce nods her head in understanding.)* I probably turned away 20 people after I was full—oh yeah, and then there was that one young couple. She was "great with child." Sweet looking young lady, real sweet.

JOYCE: Yes…what about them?

INNKEEPER: *(Sweetly.)* Oh, I let them go to the stable. I'm not an ogre, you know. *(Immediately changing moods.)* STAY ON THE WALK!! *(Joyce jumps back on the walk.)* Anyway, I told them they could stay in the stable . . . just outside the inn. I guess they did. And *(Thinking.)* that wasn't all. There was a real ruckus late last night. Well, not really a ruckus, I guess. It was actually a beautiful sound—like, well, like angels singing. And then there was some unbelievable bright light too. Now, I remember. I woke up and my whole room was as light as noonday.

JOYCE: *(Excitedly.)* Thank you! Thank you very much. I'll just run next door and see if the young couple heard the sounds and saw the light. Thanks . . . WOW—angels singing, bright light. I think maybe I've hit on something!

(Joyce exits, and the singers move to the stage again. They sing "What Child Is This?" as the nativity characters assemble. All three reporters meet at the front at center stage. Shepherd #2 is also there.)

FRED, JOYCE, and CONNIE: *(In unison, looking at one another.)* What are you two doing here???

CONNIE: *(Pointing to shepherd.)* And who's he?

FRED: I guess you could call him my guide. He's already been here once.

JOYCE: I have a very funny feeling that the Chief's hunch was right.

FRED: Me too!!!

CONNIE: I sure hope so. This is the last stop on my street beat!

(All three reporters go to the manger setting, and shepherd exits. They immediately bow reverently before the Baby Jesus. The pianist plays "O Come Let Us Adore Him.")

The reporters all rise at the conclusion of the song and return to the front of the stage.

CONNIE: You were right. That is no ordinary baby!! When I knelt by the manger it was as though I was in a royal palace. What an experience!!

FRED: Yeah! Like the angels told the shepherds, "A savior has been born who is Christ the Lord!"

CONNIE: I'll never be the same.

JOYCE: Let's get back and tell the Chief!! This is a GREAT story to tell!! He should run it on Page One.

FRED: This is the GREATEST story EVER told!!

ALL sing "Joy to the World." (All characters exit.)

Chapter 8

Too-oo-oo-oo Busy!!!

Characters/Costumes

- ❑ **Shopper #1**—Outdoor clothing
- ❑ **Shopper #2**—Outdoor clothing
- ❑ **Dan**
- ❑ **Robert**
- ❑ **Mitchell**
- ❑ **Katie**
- ❑ **Sam**
- ❑ **Mollie**
- ❑ **Garrett**
- ❑ **Jason**
- ❑ **Grocery shopper with husband**
- ❑ **Wife shopper**
- ❑ **Older students including Rachel, Gordon, and Jonathan**
- ❑ **Carolers**—All Sunday school children
- ❑ **Sunday school teacher and class**
- ❑ **Pastor**
- ❑ **Mary**—Bible-time costume (See directions on page 9 in Basics for the Director.)
- ❑ **Joseph**—Bible-time costume (See directions on page 9 in Basics for the Director.)
- ❑ **Angels**—Angel costume (See directions on page 9 in Basics for the Director.)
- ❑ **Shepherds**—Shepherd costumes (See directions on page 10 in Basics for the Director.)

Set Design/Props:

- ❑ **Lists**
- ❑ **Four tall stools or chairs**
- ❑ **Packages for shoppers**
- ❑ **Lots of grocery sacks**
- ❑ **Container of bell-shaped cookies**
- ❑ **Bible**
- ❑ **Front doors**—freezer paper or refrigerator boxes

Setting:

The stage area is decorated like a Christmas street. There are "store windows" and front doors of homes. Two women enter from the hallway carrying lots of bundles. They are both looking over their long lists (containing their scripts) as they begin their conversation.

The Play: Too-oo-oo-oo Busy!!!

Shopper #1: *(Sounding exhausted.)* Wow! This is a busy time of year! I have to shop and bake and decorate and get ready for all the parties.

Shopper #2: *(Nodding her head in agreement.)* I know what you mean. I haven't even started addressing our Christmas cards yet.

Shopper #1: *(Suddenly very excited.)* Cards?! Oh no. I knew I'd forget something. Hey, I've got to run to the store right now. I hope the cards aren't too picked over. *(She hurriedly turns around and exits.)*

Shopper #2: *(Calling after her.)* OK. See you later. I hope everything works out. *(She exits as students enter.)*

Dan: *(To his classmates.)* Have you made your Christmas list yet?

Robert: Not yet.

Dan: You'd better get started.

Mitchell: *(Enthusiastically.)* I've been working on mine!

Katie: Me too, but I ran out of space. *(She pulls her list out of her pocket and it unrolls. It is on a very long piece of adding machine tape.)*

(These four students exit. Four other students go to the front of the pulpit/stage area and sit on four tall stools. They all have "lists" too. These contain their scripts.)

Sam: People sure are busy these days.

Mollie: Yeah. Mom and Dad hardly have time to rest.

Garrett: Is that what Christmas is all about . . . being busy? I want to know.

Jason: Me too.

Sam: Let's see if we can find out what Christmas is all about. Here comes someone now. *(A couple—husband and wife—enter from the stage left. He is loaded down with packages, and she is checking things off of a long list. They move toward the kids.)* Go ask those two people, Mollie.

Mollie: *(Gets off of her stool and walks toward the couple.)* Excuse me. May I ask you a question?

Grocery Shopper: *(Not really paying attention to Mollie.)* Huh? Oh! What? Excuse me, little girl. *(To her husband.)* Isn't she cute? *(To Mollie.)* We don't have time to talk right now. *(She looks back over her list and literally turns her husband around to return to a store they must have missed. She calls over her shoulder to Mollie.)* Sorry. We're just too busy. *(To her husband.)* Isn't she cute? *(They exit into the hallway.)*

(Immediately the piano begins to play, and all Sunday school children—carolers—sing "On the First Day of Christmas." As the song begins Mollie goes back over to her stool. The four kids sit quietly pondering their dilemma. After the song is over they continue their conversation.)

Sam: We didn't find anything out from those shoppers.

Mollie: They were too busy.

Garrett: I want to know the true meaning of Christmas.

Jason: Me too!

Sam: Here comes someone else. *(Woman with lots of grocery sacks enters from the office.)* Maybe she can answer our question. *(He goes over to the woman.)* Excuse me. Are you busy?

Wife Shopper: *(Sighing, carrying grocery bag with script taped on the back of it.)* I certainly am busy. I was baking cookies, and I ran out of vanilla. I was so sure that I had plenty of vanilla. Isn't that the way it always is. The ingredient you're sure you have is the first to go. Oh yes, I'm very busy! These cookies are for church, you know. *(She pauses and thinks.)* But do you want a cookie? I do have a few from my first batch with me. *(She sets down her bags and gets a container from one sack. She hands him a cookie.)* See, they are shaped like little bells. *(She exits.)*

(Sam shrugs his shoulders and returns to his classmates at the center of the stage area. The piano plays as he returns and the carolers sing "Jingle Bells.")

Mollie: *(After the song is over.)* Well, what did she say?

Sam: She was too busy to talk.

Garrett: I want to know the true meaning of Christmas.

Jason: Me too!

Sam: Here come some older kids. They'll know what the true meaning is. They think they know EVERYTHING.

(Older students enter from hallway dressed in coats, scarves, etc. They are talking and laughing. All four younger kids go over to them and try to get their attention. The older group ignores them until they finally pull on their sleeves.)

Rachel: *(A little annoyed.)* What do you want? We're really busy.

Group: *(All chime in.)* Yeah. That's right!

Gordon: We're on our way to go caroling. We have a long list of houses to visit.

Jonathan: That's right. We've got to go. We're busy.

(They go to one of the "front doors" as the piano plays and the carolers sing "Hark the Herald Angels Sing." The four kids go back to the pulpit/stage area and get up on their stools as the song is sung.)

Sam: *(After the song is finished.)* Well, no answer yet.

Mollie: Here comes more Sunday school kids and the Sunday school teachers too.

Garrett: I want to know the true meaning of Christmas.

Jason: Me too!

(The younger students come up from the front row and are arranged by their teachers as though they are practicing the program. Individual students say verses—choose one or all.
Luke 2:11
Matthew 16:15
Isaiah 52:7
Then the carolers join the group and they all sing "Go Tell It on the Mountain.")

Teacher: Very good! Now let's go back to our seats. Later on we'll go and work on the scenery. We want to make some good looking mountains for the congregation.

Sam: Hi everyone! *(To the teacher.)* Excuse me, but we have a question. Do you know the real meaning of Christmas?

Mollie: We can't get an answer. Everyone is too busy.

Garrett: I want to know the true meaning of Christmas.

Jason: Me too!

Teacher: *(Distracted.)* Huh? What did you say? I'm sorry. We're working on the Christmas program, and we're just too busy to visit right now. Sorry.

(The teacher, class, and carolers all exit.)

Sam: Do you think we'll ever find out the true meaning of Christmas?

Mollie: Everyone is too busy!

Garrett: I want to know the true meaning of Christmas.

Jason: Me too!

(Pastor enters down the center aisle with a wreath for his office door.)

Pastor: Hi kids! How is everything going?

Mollie: Not too well.

Garrett: I'm frus-ter-ated!

Jason: Me too!

Sam: Everyone is too busy to tell us the true meaning of Christmas. We know all the regular stuff like shopping and cookies and cards, but what is the real meaning of Christmas?

Garrett: I want to know the true meaning of Christmas.

Mollie: Are you too busy too?

Pastor: Well, it is a busy time of year, but I think I've got time to talk to all of you.

Mollie: I'm glad.

Jason: Me too!

Pastor: Here let me get my Bible *(script inside)*. It's all in God's Word. *(He reads Luke 2:1-14 and as he reads, the nativity characters enter and pose.)*

All carolers sing "Silent Night."

Pastor: God sent His Son to earth at Christmas. Jesus lived on this earth for 33 years, and then He was crucified. It was really sad, but it was all part of God's plan. Jesus never did anything wrong. He didn't die for HIS sins, He died for our sins. He was the perfect sacrifice. And the Bible says in Romans 10:9-10 *(He reads from his Bible.)*. Then we can spend eternity in heaven with God. *(He pauses and then continues.)* So the busyness and fun is a part of the celebration of Christmas. We just have to be cautious that being busy doesn't replace being with Christ. Jesus is what it is all about. He is the true meaning of Christmas.

Jason: Jesus came to earth . . . so that we could go to heaven!! Jesus is the true meaning of Christmas. *(Very excited!)* I get it!! I get it!!

All 3 kids: Me too!!

All carolers sing "Joy to the World."

Chapter 9

Happy Birthday, Jesus

Characters/Costumes:

- ❑ **Early-bird guest**—Dressed for birthday party. (This character must be capable and comfortable adlibbing lines.)
- ❑ **Angel**—Angel costume (See directions on page 9 in Basics for the Director.)
- ❑ **Mary**—Bible-time costume (See directions on page 9 in Basics for the Director.)
- ❑ **Joseph**—Bible-time costume (See directions on page 9 in Basics for the Director.)
- ❑ **Jesus**—Doll or baby

Set Design/Props:

- ❑ **Room decorated with balloons and a "Happy Birthday" banner**
- ❑ **Christmas tree**
- ❑ **Large wrapped presents** (whose lids will lift off or up)—one for each class
- ❑ **Oatmeal box drums**
- ❑ **Birthday cake** (optional)

Setting:

A living room with a Christmas tree and large wrapped presents. The room is decorated with colorful balloons and a "Happy Birthday" banner (maybe even a cake with candles). One early bird arrives before the party is ready to begin and before the other guests. The early bird is pleased to be there, but is pretty "nosy." She carries on a mumbling monologue as she peeks and pokes at each package.

The Play: Happy Birthday, Jesus

Early bird: *(Looking at first package.)* **This is a pretty package. I wonder what is inside.** *(Moving to the next box.)* **This is really interesting!** *(Next box.)* **Wow! Look how big this package is!** *(Glancing at the Happy Birthday Banner.)* **Happy birthday . . . Hmmmm! Whose birthday is it?**

(Finally she can stand it no longer, and she starts to peek inside the boxes. As she opens the lid of each box and looks in, different classes come up on stage, and beginning with the youngest class first, they "sing" their present for the Christ-child.)

You can add or delete classes as needed for your group of children. You can also change the songs to ones that are favorites of the children in your church.

Youngest class: "Ho, Ho, Ho Hosanna"

2nd class: "Little Drummer Boy" *(make oatmeal drums)*

3rd class: "Go Tell It on the Mountain"

Oldest class: "What Child Is This?"

Early bird: *(The early-bird comments are made before and after lifting each box lid and hearing the song.)* **"Oh, I probably shouldn't be doing this"** . . . **"Just one little peek"** . . . etc., etc.

When all the gifts are open, the early-bird guest continues . . .

Early bird: **But who is going to receive all these presents? Who is having a birthday?**

(All the classes come up on stage and sing "Happy Birthday, Jesus." As they sing, the actors in the nativity scene assemble on stage in front of the children who have been singing. After "Happy Birthday, Jesus" concludes, the attention shifts to the nativity scene, and the piano plays softly. The angel reads Luke 2:1-14. At the conclusion, the congregation all sing "Silent Night.")

Early Bird: *(In closing.)* I get it! Happy Birthday! Happy Birthday, Jesus, and Merry Christmas to everyone!

Chapter 10

I Didn't Think It Would Happen Like This!!

Characters/Costumes

- ❑ **Linda**
- ❑ **Rich**
- ❑ **Singers**
- ❑ **Pharisees #1, #2, #3**—Bible-time costumes (See directions on page 9 in Basics for the Director.)
- ❑ **Aaron**
- ❑ **Chad**
- ❑ **Kyle**
- ❑ **Mary**—Bible-time costume (See directions on page 9 in Basics for the Director.)
- ❑ **Joseph**—Bible-time costume (See directions on page 9 in Basics for the Director.)
- ❑ **Angel**—Angel costume (See directions on page 9 in Basics for the Director.)
- ❑ **Shepherds**—Shepherd costumes (See directions on page 10 in Basics for the Director.)

Set Design/Props:

- ❑ **Scrolls**
- ❑ **Manger**
- ❑ **Stool**
- ❑ **Christmas tree with lights** (unlit)
- ❑ **Doll**—to represent baby Jesus

Setting:

On stage there is a stool and an unlit Christmas tree.

The Play: I Didn't Think It Would Happen Like This!!

Linda: *(Offstage with a microphone, in a determined voice.)* Come on, Rich. Go out there! The script says that the narrator's cue is the ending of the prelude. It's over! *(More excited.)* Go out there! *(In a loud stage whisper to the pianist.)* Pssst!! Overture!

Pianist: *(Plays a rousing overture of some Christmas tunes . . . midway through she turns around to see no one on stage and immediately gets softer, then stops abruptly.)*

Rich: *(Still off stage and just as determined as Linda.)* No way!! Did you look out there? There are no kids on stage. There's no manger or shepherds. The Christmas tree isn't even lit! What's going on? *(A little dismayed.)* I didn't think it would happen like this!!

Linda: *(Annoyed and confused.)* Who knows. There must be a little problem. *(Brightening a little.)* I know, a technical difficulty. *(Discouraged once again.)* I don't know. All I know is that the end of the prelude is supposed to signal your entrance. Now go!! *(In a loud stage whisper.)* Pssst!! *(To the piano player.)* Overture!

Pianist: *(Smiles with relief, plays loudly, and then turns to see no one on stage. Once again she stops abruptly and looks around nervously.)*

Rich: *(Exasperated.)* I'm not going out there! When I volunteered to be the narrator, I didn't think it would happen like this! Where is everyone? Where is everything?

Linda: *(Totally distraught.)* I don't know. *(Regaining her determination.)* But you've got to get this program started!

Rich: *(Puzzled.)* What program? I feel like the Lone Ranger. What should I say?

Linda: *(Thinking.)* Well, just welcome the folks here tonight . . . and then fake it! *(In a very loud stage whisper.)* Pssst!! *(To piano player.)* Overture! *(To Rich.)* Now get going!!

Pianist: *(Plays much less robustly, turns and sees Rich entering, being pushed on stage by Linda. Pianist sighs as she plays with more confidence once again, and the volume increases to the completion of the overture.)*

Rich: *(Onstage now and obviously flustered. He walks to the stool and picks up the microphone and reads.)* Uh, welcome!! Welcome, ladies and gentlemen. Welcome to our Christmas program. *(Stops reading.)* We're having a few small problems this evening *(He pauses and remembers Linda's words.)* . . . some technical difficulties. But I'm sure that they'll be cleared up soon. Then things will be moving along. In the meantime . . . uh, ah, OH! I see we have some lovely decorations here on stage . . . and they haven't been lit yet. Let me go over and see if I can turn on the lights of this beautiful tree. *(Rich goes over to the tree and hunts and fiddles. He turns and shouts to the audience.)* Please excuse me. I am going backstage to make a few minor adjustments. Thank you for your understanding and patience. *(In a very loud stage whisper)* Pssst!! *(To the piano player.)* Play something, anything!

Pianist: *(Plays "We Need a Little Christmas" . . . quietly at first.)*

Rich: *(Offstage.)* How embarrassing! I didn't think it would happen like this!!

Pianist: *(Plays much louder and the younger elementary kids come up to the stage. After everyone is in place, they sing "We Need a Little Christmas." After the song, the kids return to their seats and Pharisees enter.)*

Pharisee #1: I don't know what's wrong! As the religious leaders of this nation, we ought to know a little more about when the Messiah will arrive.

Pharisee #2: Well, Isaiah gave us some information, but things are still a little hazy.

Pharisee #1: Yes, he said that. *(Reads Isaiah 7:14 and then Psalm 132:11 from the scroll.)*

Pharisee #2: That's right! And Micah said *(Reading from the scroll.)* that he would come out of Bethlehem. *(Looking up.)* Since we're here in Bethlehem, we should be the first to see the prophesy fulfilled.

Pharisee #3: *(With enthusiasm.)* Personally, *(Imagining the scene.)* I can see Him descending from the heavens with a celestial choir and orchestra as a back-up group.

Pharisee #1: *(Equally enthusiastic.)* Not me, I see Him entering the city on a swift and mighty steed . . . thundering into the city with sword brandished and fire in His eyes.

Pharisee #2: I think either one of those things is possible. I just wish we didn't have to wait and wait. I didn't think it would happen like this!

Pharisees #1 and #3: I didn't either!

(The Pharisees "freeze action" on the stage and the pianist plays "What Child Is This?" As she plays, the younger elementary children return to the stage as do Mary, carrying Baby Jesus, and Joseph. Mary, Joseph, Baby Jesus, and the angel "freeze" in the typical manger scene. When everyone is settled, lecture lights are lit, and the kids sing "Away in a Manger." All remain in place.)

Angel: Reads Luke 2:1-18

(Singers exit as the shepherds join the Pharisees. They pantomime telling these "religious leaders" about the birth of Jesus. Then the shepherds exit.)

Pharisee #1: (Aloud.) What?

Pharisee #2: In a manger? In a stable?

Pharisee #3: Christ the Lord?

Pharisee #1,2, and 3: I didn't think it would happen like this! (They all exit, shaking their heads in disbelief.)

Linda: (Offstage, oblivious to what has been happening.) Rich, I don't know where the switch is. Are you sure that it wasn't out there on the Christmas tree?

Rich: I'm sure! I looked! OHHHHHH (Moaning.) I didn't think it would happen like this!

Linda: *(A little disgusted.)* Happen, smappen. You've got to get out there on stage and DO something!

Rich: Do something? What would you suggest I do? Sing? Dance? Tell funny stories?

Linda: *(Emphatically.)* NO! It's been a bad enough night already!! Just go out there and tell everyone you're sorry . . . after all, *(Mocking just a little.)* "You didn't think it would happen like this" . . . and then wish them a Merry Christmas.

Rich: Oh, how embarrassing. I suppose I could say something, only PLEASE don't ask for the overture again.

Linda: I won't. It's far too late for that.

Rich: *(Walks back on to stage and picks up the mike. Fumbling, he reads from notes.)* Uh, hi again folks. I really want to thank you for coming tonight, and I'm really sorry that our "technical difficulties" were never resolved *(He glances at the unlit tree.)* Anyway, it was great to have you here. You've been a terrific audience. *(Pleadingly.)* Honest folks, I didn't think it would happen like this!

Pianist: *(Begins to play softly "We Need a Little Christmas.")*

Rich: So . . . well . . . we'll see you again next Christmas *(Under his breath.)* I mean someone else will see you . . . I'll never take THIS job again. (Louder.) and until then . . .

Pianist: *(Plays a little louder as the younger elementary children go back up on stage.)*

Rich: *(Surprised to see the kids.)* Hey, kids, wait!! What are you doing? Where were you a little while ago? What's going on?

Younger elementary kids: (Recite together Isaiah 9:6. One of the younger kids then goes over by the Christmas tree and stamps his foot. Immediately the tree lights come on. [Someone plugs them in.])

Rich: *(Looks at the beautiful lights in disbelief.)*

Aaron: *(Pointing to Rich.)* He didn't think it would happen like this!

Chad: But it's not the first time people were surprised at Christmas. And it won't be the last.

ALL actors and participants: MERRY CHRISTMAS!

All (can be just the participants or the entire congregation) sing "Joy to the World."

Chapter 11

Footprints to the Manger

Characters/Costumes:

- ❏ **Mindy**—Outdoor clothing
- ❏ **Patty**—Outdoor clothing
- ❏ **Elisa**—Outdoor clothing
- ❏ **Mary**—Bible-time costume (See directions on page 9 in Basics for the Director.)
- ❏ **Joseph**—Bible-time costume (See directions on page 9 in Basics for the Director.)
- ❏ **Shepherds**—Shepherd costumes (See directions on page 10 in Basics for the Director.)
- ❏ **Angels**—Angel costume (See directions on page 9 in Basics for the Director.)

Set Design/Props:

- ❏ **Artificial snow is optional**
- ❏ **Large footprints**
- ❏ **Manger**

Setting:

Winter scene, out-of-doors with lots of snow. Three kids are playing in the snow and enjoying the fun . . .

The Play: Footprints to the Manger

Mindy: *(Enters skipping through the snow.)* What a terrific day! I love it when it snows!

Patty: *(Following Mindy.)* Me, too! Can you believe those big drifts? When I woke up this morning and looked outside I was really surprised!

Elisa: So was I! The weatherman said snow, but I had no idea it would be so much . . . or so beautiful!

Mindy: *(Very excited.)* Let's have a snowball fight! Let's build a snowman!! Let's . . . let's make a fort! Let's . . .

Elisa: *(Interrupting.)* Whoa! We can't do everything at once. *(Smiles at Mindy's enthusiasm.)*

Mindy: You're right. Let's make snow angels. Do you know how to make snow angels? *(She lies down and illustrates while she explains.)* See? You lie down on the fresh snow and move your arms and legs to make patterns.

Patty: I'm going to try that. Boy, it sure is easy to find fresh snow today. We're the first ones out here after the big snowfall! *(Lies down in snow. So does Elisa).*

Mindy: *(Hops up and goes to look at Patty's angel.)* That's beautiful! *(Turning to Elisa.)* Yours is great, too!

Patty: *(Goes over to Elisa's angel and then wanders away. Suddenly she starts shouting!)* Speaking of patterns in the snow, take a look at this footprint. It is really unusual. Over here . . . come and look! *(She moves slightly to stage right.)*

Elisa: That is different!

(Freeze action.) The next lines are taped on the floor for review.

Youngest Sunday school class walks up to the stage and stands on the far right. They recite Proverbs 13:20a in unison. Then they sing "Jesus Loves Me." (Exit.)

Elisa: *(Action resumes.)* Did you hear that? It seemed to be coming from over there. *(Points to the far right. Patty wanders away again.)*

Mindy: I thought maybe I might have heard some singing, but I'm not sure.

Patty: *(Excitedly.)* Wow!! Another footprint! *(A little farther to the right.)* Look! Over here . . . it's similar to that last one and really different from our footprints. *(Mindy and Elisa go to look.)*

(Freeze action.) The lines for next segment are taped on floor. The next older class goes up to stage and recites one or more of the following Bible verses.
Psalm 1:1a
Isaiah 2:5
Isaiah 30:21b
1 John 1:7a

After reciting one or more verses, they sing "Go Tell It on the Mountain." (They exit.)

Elisa: Did you hear that? I heard voices and singing. It was coming from up ahead of us. Did you hear it? *(Again pointing right.)*

Mindy: I think I did. I mean I thought I did. I mean . . . I don't know. How about you, Patty?

Patty: Yes, I definitely heard something. *(Wanders away while talking.)* And I think that it had to do with these strange footprints. Look! Here's another one. *(Even farther right.)*

(Freeze action.) The lines for the next segment are taped on the floor. The next age level goes up to pulpit/stage area and children recite one or more of these verses.
Micah 6:8
John 8:12
2 John :6

After reciting one or more verses, they sing "Silent Night."
(Then Exit.)

Elisa: *(Action resumes.)* Now you had to hear that! There was singing, and I heard some terrific verses too!

Mindy: I heard it too! It was really interesting. I heard poems about how God wants us to behave.

Patty: Yes! How He wants us to walk . . . what we should do to please Him. *(Walks away a little.)* And here's another footprint!

Elisa: They're all leading this direction. *(She points toward the pulpit/stage area.)*

(Freeze action.) Mary and Joseph, with Baby Jesus and an angel enter reverently and freeze on far right. When the scene is set, the angel reads from Luke 2:1-14.

Elisa: *(Action resumes.)* **Did you hear that?**

Mindy: And see that?

Patty: I sure did. Those footprints we've been finding and following have led to the manger—the manger where the Christ child was born.

Elisa: Those verses all talked about the way God wants us to walk.

Patty: If we follow those footprints, we'll come closer and closer to the manger.

Mindy: And we'll come closer to Jesus!

All sing "Joy to the World."

Ornaments of Christmas

Characters/Costumes:

- ❏ **Elizabeth**
- ❏ **Mitchell**
- ❏ **Teacher**
- ❏ **Katie**
- ❏ **Jackie**
- ❏ **Keri**
- ❏ **Mollie**
- ❏ **Garrett**
- ❏ **Chad**
- ❏ **Marissa**

Set Design/Props:

- ❏ **Nativity scene under the tree**
- ❏ **A large cardboard box labeled "ORNAMENTS"**
- ❏ **Ornaments** (Need to be large and exaggerated and include several candy canes, several bells, and an angel.)
- ❏ **A tree decorated** with the above ornaments and placed on the stage
- ❏ **Doll to represent baby Jesus**

Setting:

A decorated Christmas tree is in the center of the stage. A big box labeled "ORNAMENTS" is sitting beside the tree.

The Play: Ornaments of Christmas

All the children enter singing "Super Duper Christmas" in the past tense. ("We had a super duper Christmas.") When they are done singing, they can sit down near the tree.

Elizabeth: *(Sadly.)* Oh boy, I can't believe Christmas is ~~Here~~/over. ~~The next thing you know, school will be starting again.~~

Mitchell: *(Solemnly.)* Yeah, I've already started the count. *Christmas day is in* ~~School will start in~~ 7 days, 22 hours, 42 minutes, and 56 seconds. Make that 54 seconds, 53 second, 52, 51 . . .

I'LL miss my teacher @ school

Elizabeth: *(Perking up.)* ~~It will be fun to see my teacher. I miss her . . . (Pause.).~~

Mitchell: *(Looking around.)* Speaking of teachers . . . I wonder where our Sunday school teacher is. Do you think she might have gotten lost in the holiday shuffle?

Teacher: *(Entering, looking a little disheveled. She's carrying another box labeled "ORNAMENTS." Her lines are taped to the side.)* Here I am . . . I had the hardest time finding my shoes. I thought someone threw them out with the used wrapping paper. Are you ready to ~~take the Christmas decorations down?~~ *put up the christmas decorations*

All: OK!

Teacher: Now where should we start? I know, let's start with the candy canes. Would someone please take a candy cane from the tree?

Katie: *(Katie takes a candy cane from the ~~tree~~.)* [Box]

[omit] **Teacher:** Can any of you tell me what you think of when you see a candy cane? *(Several students hold their hands up for the teacher to call on them. She points to five children and they go to center stage.)*

Katie: *(Holding the candy cane.)* The candy cane is hard. That's to remind us that Jesus is our solid rock. *(She passes the candy cane to the next student.)*

Jackie: The big red stripe stands for the blood that was shed by Jesus on the cross. *(She passes the cane to the next child.)*

Keri: There are three small stripes. That's to remind us of the beating that Jesus took for us when they beat Him. It is by His stripes that we are healed. *(Cane is passed.)*

Mollie: The white shows us the sinless nature of Jesus. Jesus never sinned. *(Cane is passed.)*

Garrett: The candy cane is shaped like the hook that the shepherds use to save a lost lamb. Jesus reaches down to save us when we go astray. *(Pause.)* And look! If you turn it upside down it is the letter *J*.

[omit] **Teacher:** *(Pleased with her students.)* That's very good. Can you tell me what the letter *J* is for?

Katie: *J* is for Jesus and *J* is for joy.

Jackie: Jesus give us joy.

omit **Teacher:** Let's sing a song about joy!

Elizabeth and Mitchell: Let's sing "Joy to the World!"

(All sing! And several kids remove all the candy canes from the tree and put them into the "ORNAMENTS" box.)

Teacher: That was very good! Will someone get a bell?
Box
(Chad goes to tree and takes a bell from it.) What do you think of when you see a bell?

(The kids all raise their hands to show that they know the answer. The teacher calls on two of them. They move to center stage.)

Chad: (Holding the bell.)
The bells rang out a message
Of a manger filled with hay
Where God's Son, baby Jesus
Was born on Christmas Day.
(Passes the bell to Marissa.)

Marissa: (Holding the bell.)
Bells ring out at Christmas
To celebrate His birth.
Jesus is the King
Who came from heaven to earth.

Teacher: Let's sing a song about bells.

Elizabeth and Mitchell: Let's sing "Come on Ring Those Bells."

(All sing "Come On Ring Those Bells" and all the bells are removed from the tree and put into the "ORNAMENTS" box.)
on the Tree

Teacher: There is just one thing left on the tree. Who can get it down for me? *(Mitchell takes the angel from the tree and hands the angel to the teacher.)* The angels played a very special part the night that Jesus was born. Do you know what it was?

(Several students raise their hands, and the teacher calls on Keri.)

Keri: The angels' happy voices sang of "peace, good will on earth." They told the shepherds in the field of the dear Savior's birth.

Teacher: Let's sing a song about angels.

Elizabeth and Mitchell: Let's sing "Angels We Have Heard on High."

(All sing as teacher puts the angel in the box.)

Mollie: Look at our tree now. It's all empty.
It's all done

omit **Garrett:** Wait, the nativity scene is still under the tree. Can we leave that out? Can we leave it out?

omit **Teacher:** Sure we can! Just because Christmas is over doesn't mean we can't keep celebrating. We can celebrate the birth of Jesus everyday! And we can tell others of His love.

omit **Elizabeth:** Let's sing a song about . . . about . . .

 **Mitchell:** about telling others!

 **Elizabeth and Mitchell:** Let's sing "Go Tell It on the Mountain."

(All sing "Go Tell It on the Mountain," and then everyone sings "We Wish You a Merry Christmas.")

The Word at Work Around the World

What would you do if you wanted to share God's love with children on the streets of your city? That's the dilemma David C. Cook faced in 1870's Chicago. His answer was to create literature that would capture children's hearts.

Out of those humble beginnings grew a worldwide ministry that has used literature to proclaim God's love and disciple generation after generation. Cook Communications Ministries is committed to personal discipleship—to helping people of all ages learn God's Word, embrace His salvation, walk in His ways, and minister in His name.

Faith Kidz, RiverOak, Honor, Life Journey, Victor, NextGen . . . every time you purchase a book produced by Cook Communications Ministries, you not only meet a vital personal need in your life or in the life of someone you love, but you're also a part of ministering to José in Colombia, Humberto in Chile, Gousa in India, or Lidiane in Brazil. You help make it possible for a pastor in China, a child in Peru, or a mother in West Africa to enjoy a life-changing book. And because you helped, children and adults around the world are learning God's Word and walking in His ways.

Thank you for your partnership in helping to disciple the world. May God bless you with the power of His Word in your life.

For more information about our international ministries, visit www.ccmi.org.